MW01610831

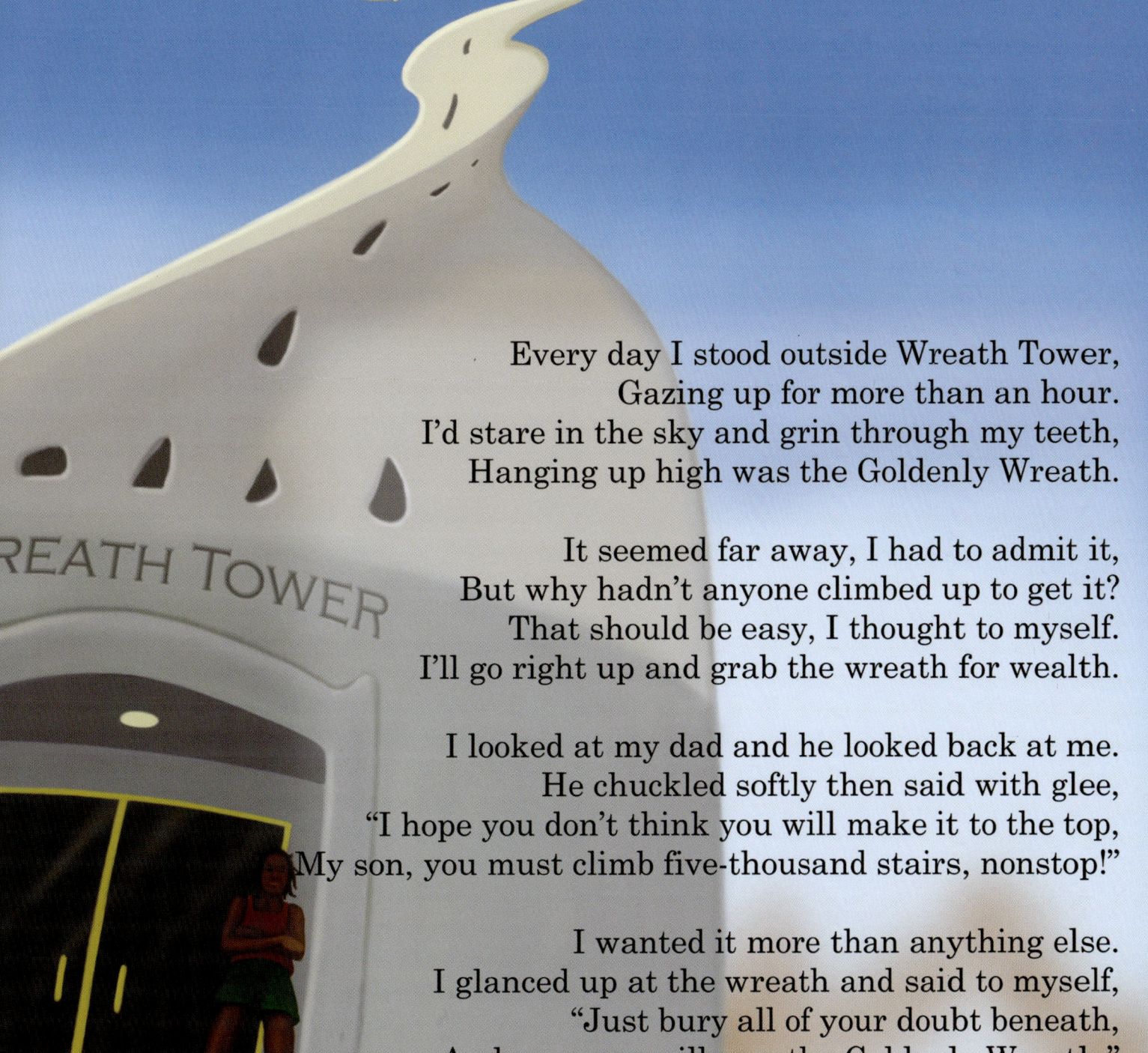

Every day I stood outside Wreath Tower,
Gazing up for more than an hour.
I'd stare in the sky and grin through my teeth,
Hanging up high was the Goldenly Wreath.

It seemed far away, I had to admit it,
But why hadn't anyone climbed up to get it?
That should be easy, I thought to myself.
I'll go right up and grab the wreath for wealth.

I looked at my dad and he looked back at me.
He chuckled softly then said with glee,
"I hope you don't think you will make it to the top,
My son, you must climb five-thousand stairs, nonstop!"

I wanted it more than anything else.
I glanced up at the wreath and said to myself,
"Just bury all of your doubt beneath,
And soon you will own the Goldenly Wreath."

We walked away, but I kept looking back.
The wreath would be mine, and that was a fact.

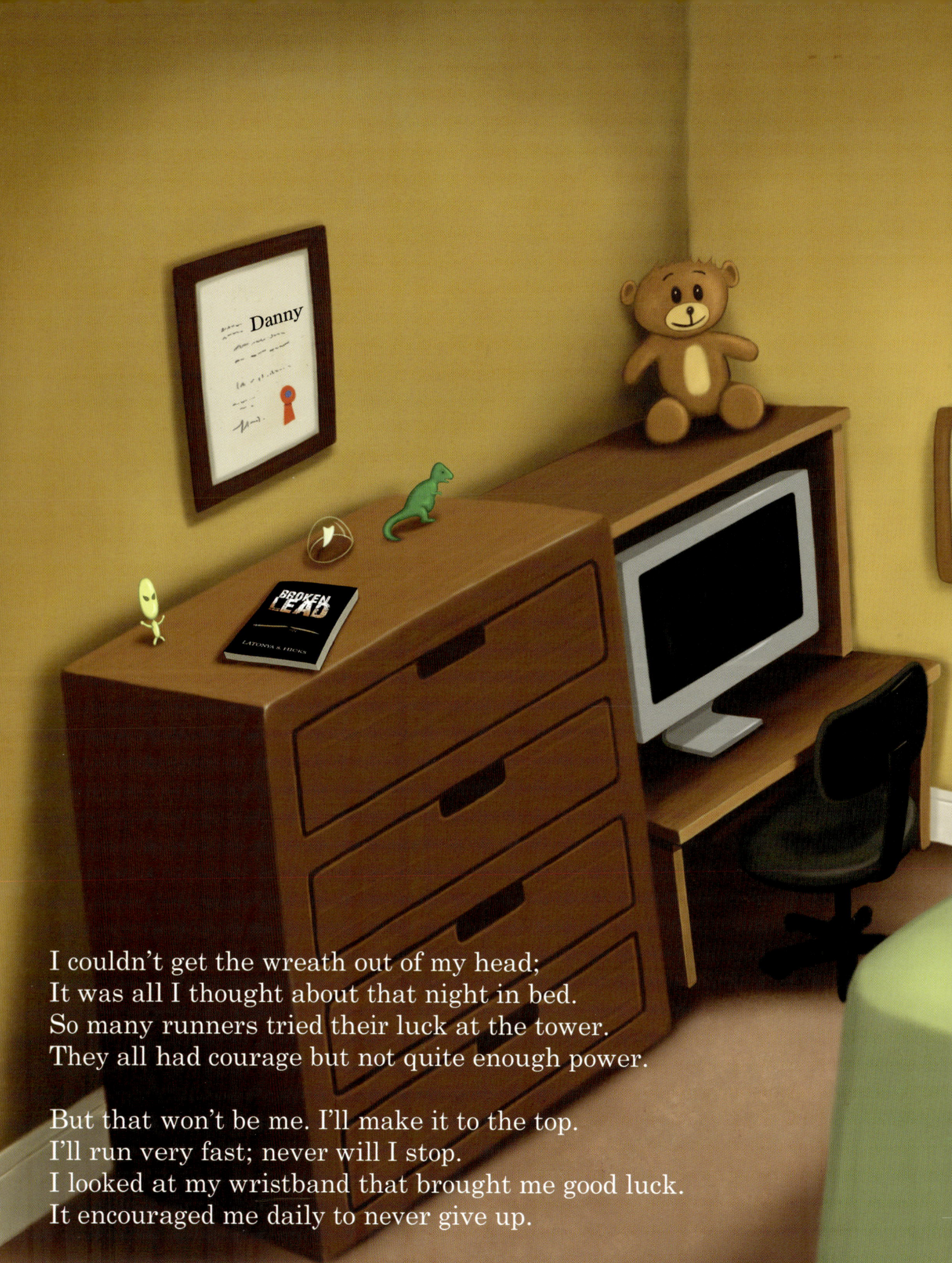

I couldn't get the wreath out of my head;
It was all I thought about that night in bed.
So many runners tried their luck at the tower.
They all had courage but not quite enough power.

But that won't be me. I'll make it to the top.
I'll run very fast; never will I stop.
I looked at my wristband that brought me good luck.
It encouraged me daily to never give up.

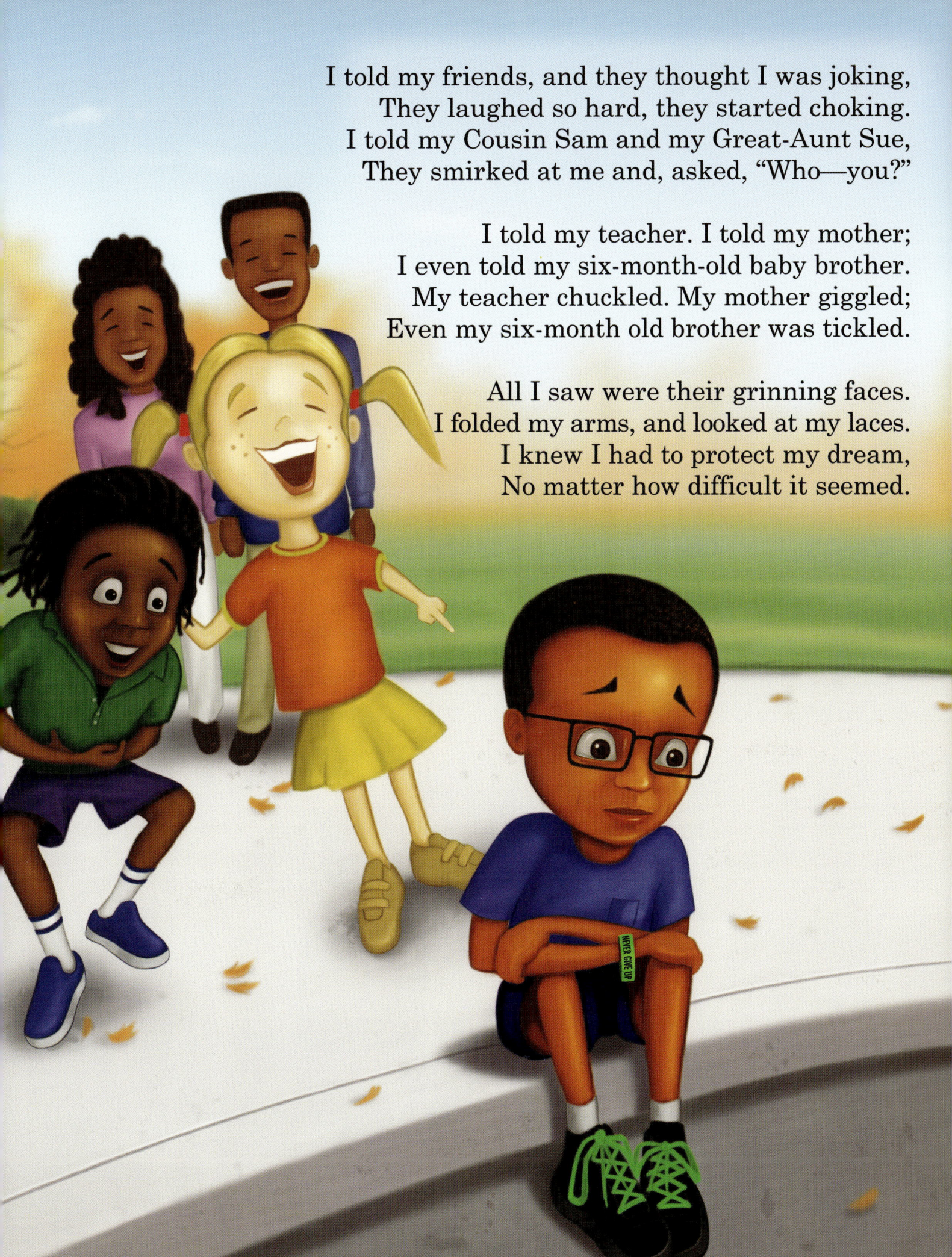

I told my friends, and they thought I was joking,
They laughed so hard, they started choking.
I told my Cousin Sam and my Great-Aunt Sue,
They smirked at me and, asked, "Who—you?"

I told my teacher. I told my mother;
I even told my six-month-old baby brother.
My teacher chuckled. My mother giggled;
Even my six-month old brother was tickled.

All I saw were their grinning faces.
I folded my arms, and looked at my laces.
I knew I had to protect my dream,
No matter how difficult it seemed.

Every day for the next year,
I lifted weights to get my body in gear.
I ate on the run. I'd dash and I'd hustle.
My body bulked up with mass and muscle.

Nothing was going to stand in my way,
And I did not care what anyone would say.
I could run like a cheetah and leap like a locust.
I had to work hard; I had to stay focused.

I'd look up at the wreath time after time.
I'd point at it and say, "You're mine!"

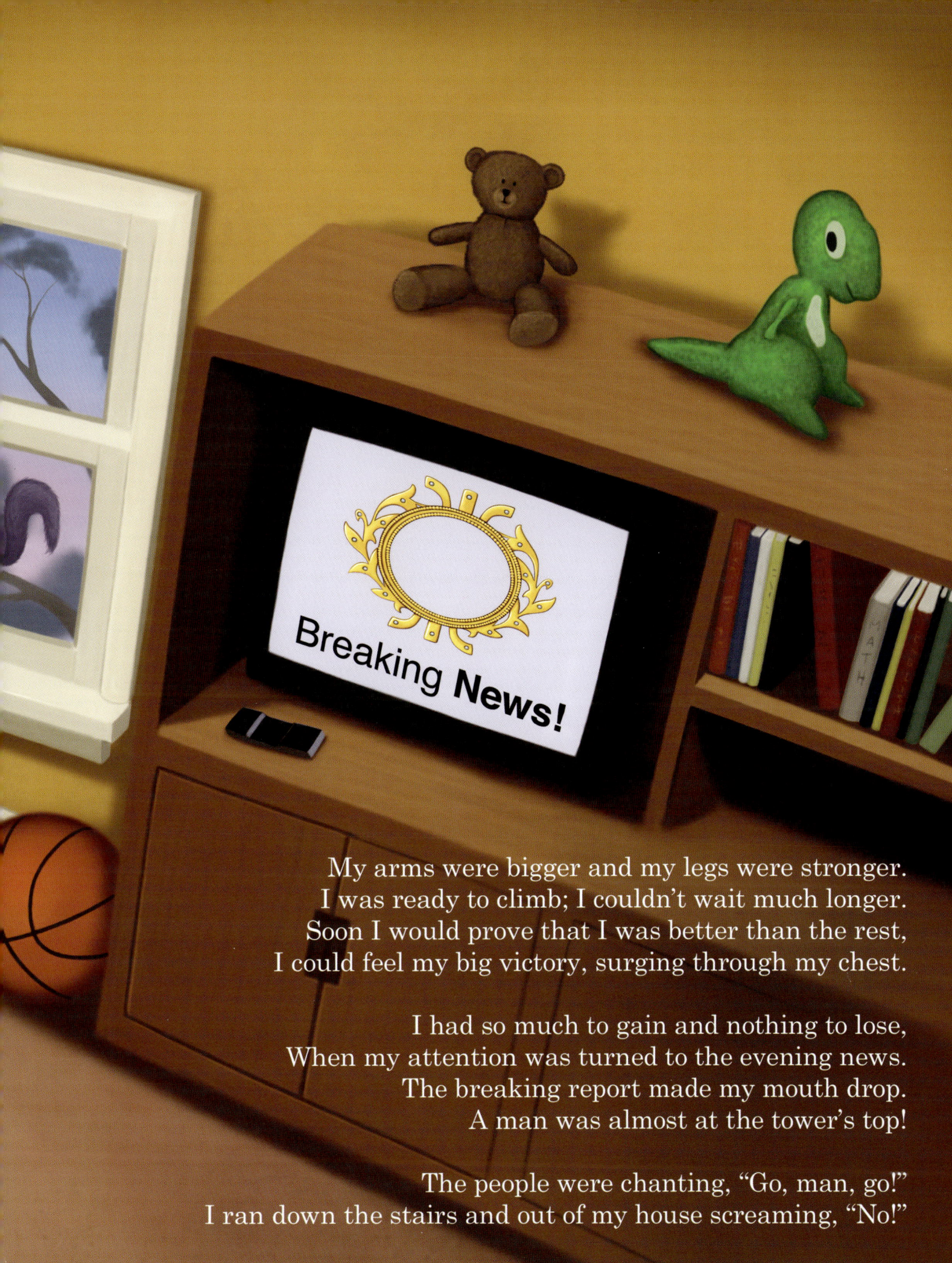

My arms were bigger and my legs were stronger.
I was ready to climb; I couldn't wait much longer.
Soon I would prove that I was better than the rest,
I could feel my big victory, surging through my chest.

I had so much to gain and nothing to lose,
When my attention was turned to the evening news.
The breaking report made my mouth drop.
A man was almost at the tower's top!

The people were chanting, "Go, man, go!"
I ran down the stairs and out of my house screaming, "No!"

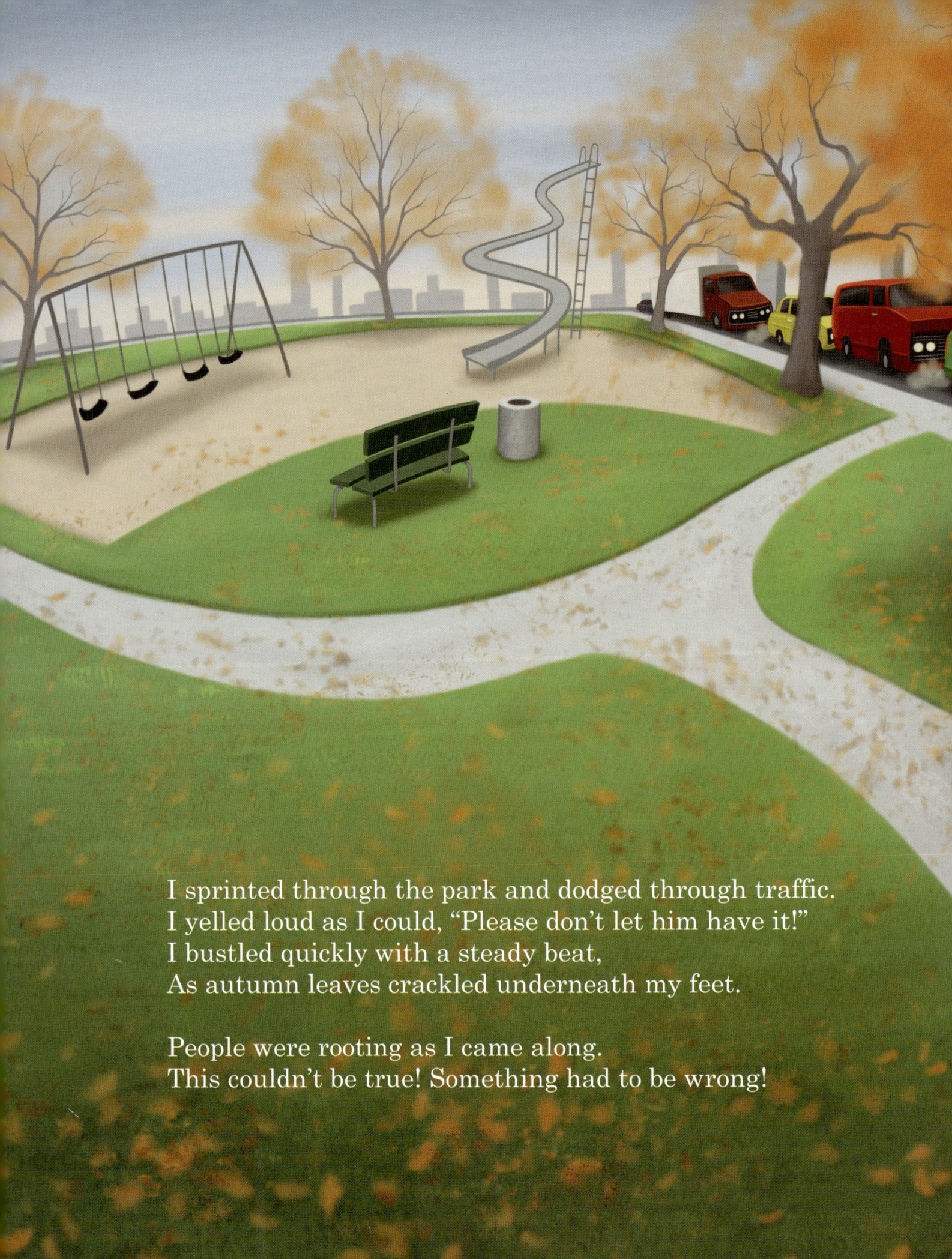

I sprinted through the park and dodged through traffic.
I yelled loud as I could, "Please don't let him have it!"
I bustled quickly with a steady beat,
As autumn leaves crackled underneath my feet.

People were rooting as I came along.
This couldn't be true! Something had to be wrong!

When I made it to the building, I knew it was too late,
The runner's big victory had sealed my fate.
Everyone was standing jolly and free.
Tears filled my eyes; that was supposed to be me!

My joy was gone. My dream had been crushed.
I couldn't even think. My mind was mush.
I felt so empty. I let myself down.
I glanced at my wrist and started to frown.

For the next five minutes, no one made a sound.
We all waited by the tower for the man to come down.
The town was silent, as were the leaves on the trees,
I almost collapsed and fell to my knees.

Then I heard a rattle, a shake at the door.
The footsteps grew closer as they padded across the floor.

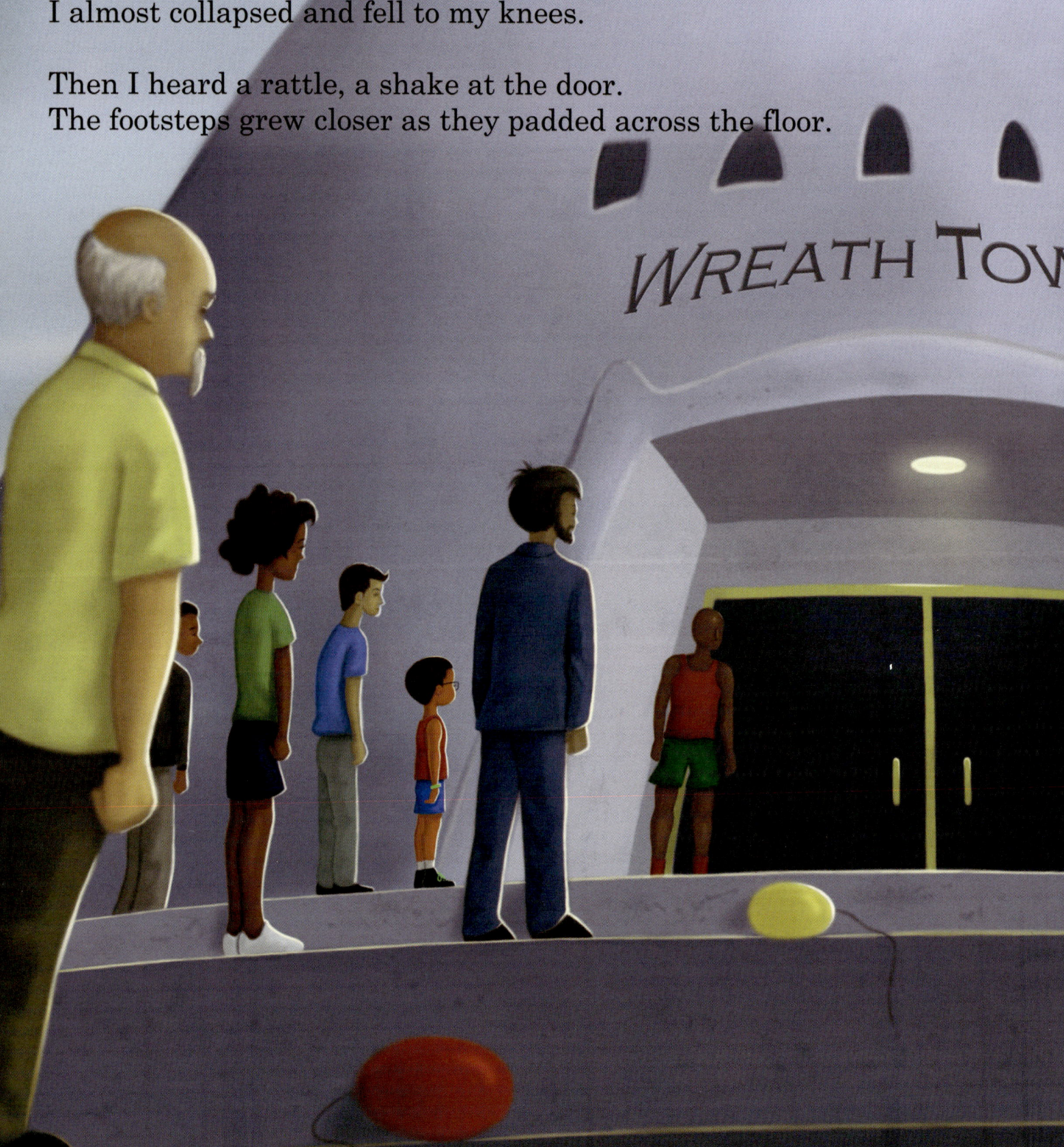

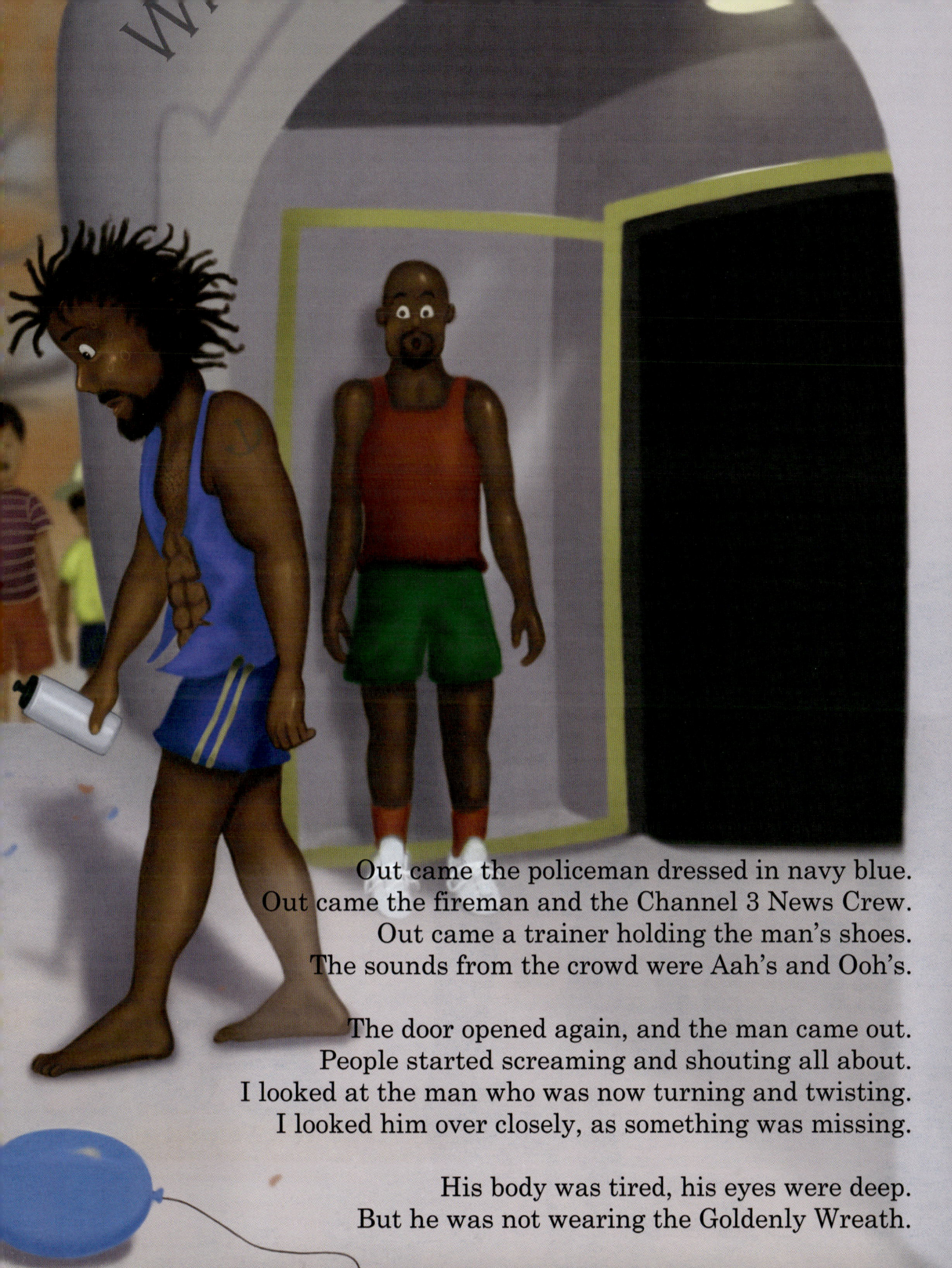

Out came the policeman dressed in navy blue.
Out came the fireman and the Channel 3 News Crew.
Out came a trainer holding the man's shoes.
The sounds from the crowd were Aah's and Ooh's.

The door opened again, and the man came out.
People started screaming and shouting all about.
I looked at the man who was now turning and twisting.
I looked him over closely, as something was missing.

His body was tired, his eyes were deep.
But he was not wearing the Goldenly Wreath.

The police began to yell on their megaphones,
"Everyone please, go back to your homes!"
Did the man win? I slowly pondered.
Where was the wreath, I wondered.

I huffed and puffed and hung my head,
But then the anchorman slowly said,
"With only one final stair left to climb,
The runner gave up at stair 4,999."

The crowd was stunned, and so was I.
But now I'd get my chance to give it a try.
I looked at my wristband, which brought me good luck.
It encouraged me daily to never give up.

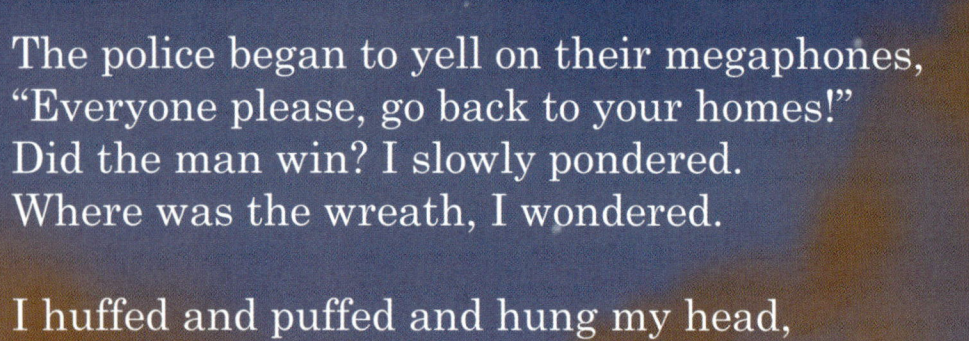

The next day, I arrived at the tower for the race.
My heart was beating at a rapid pace.
The tower guard yelled, "Who's next to try?"
I raised my hand with confidence and said, "I."

He sneered and jeered to put me down,
"Beat it, kid! Stop playing around!"
Spectators yelled as I changed my stance,
"He can run, just give him a chance!"

He walked over to me. His voice was low.
"All right kid, when I say go, then go."
The look in his eyes was very cunning,
But at the sound of his voice, I took off running.

Step two, step three, step four, and step five,
Step six, step seven, I started to strive.
I ran up each step even quicker than the last.
I was stronger than strong and faster than fast.

Stair after stair, pound after pound,
I thought I could fly I was so high off the ground.
My left foot shivered; there was pain in my shin.
Then the pain vanished as I got my second wind.

I wanted so badly to win the gold,
In spite of the negative things I'd been told.
I kept picturing everyone's faces of laughter,
And I just kept running faster and faster.

I lifted my wrist to touch the wristband I wore.
Then I looked straight ahead and fixed my eyes on the door.

I opened the door with a grin through my teeth,
And there it hung, the Goldenly Wreath.
I peered over the tower; my body was rigid.
A man yelled and pointed, "Look, that darn kid did it!"

The wreath shined just like I'd imagined it would;
I had accomplished my dream and it felt so good.
Even though people laughed at my dream, it came true,
Because I can do anything that I put my mind to!

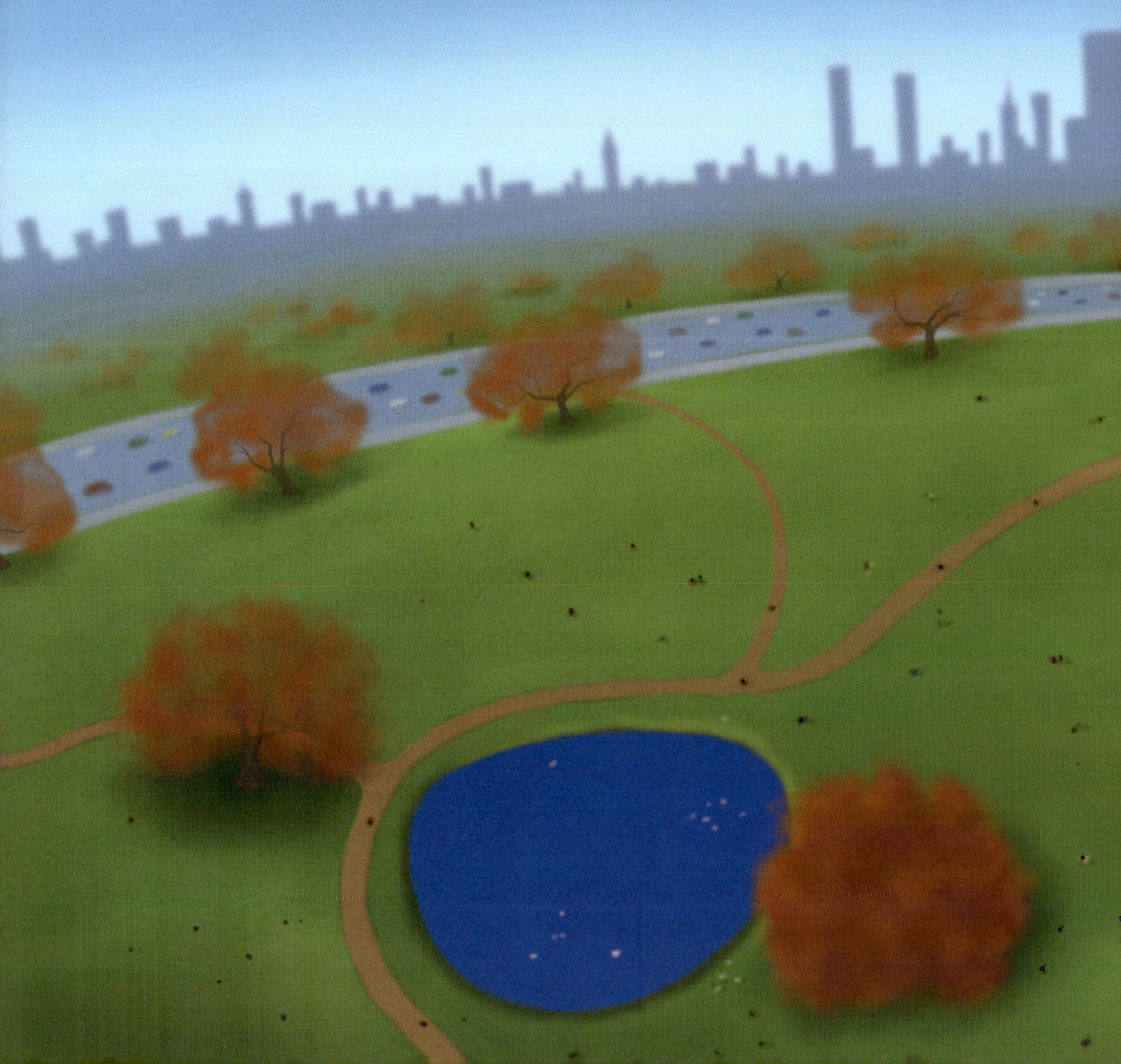

Latonya S. Hicks graduated from Purdue University. She is a member of the Society of Children's Book Writers and Illustrators. The Goldenly Wreath is her first children's book. She lives in Indiana and is currently working on her second children's book. Visit www.thegoldenlywreath.com for exciting news about the book.

Illustrator Steve Feldman works from his studio in northeast Oregon. He is a PAL member of SCBWI. More of his work can be seen at www.stevefeldman.com